W9-CKQ-783

OUTDOOR SPACES

Design
Is in the
Details

Brad Mee

Sterling Publishing Co., Inc. New York
A Sterling/Chapelle Book

Chapelle, Limited

Jo Packham
Sara Toliver
Cindy Stoeckl

Editor: Karmen Quinney
Copy Editor: Marilyn Goff
Design/Layout: Brad Mee
Cover Image: Jessie Walker

If you have any questions or comments, please contact:
Chapelle, Ltd., Inc., P.O. Box 9252 Ogden, UT 84409
(801) 621-2777 • FAX (801) 621-2788
• e-mail: chapelle@chapelleltd.com
• web site: www.chapelleltd.com

The photographs and written text in this volume are intended
for the personal use of the reader and may be reproduced for that
purpose only. Any other use, especially commercial use, is for-
bidden under law without the written permission of the copyright
holder. Every effort has been made to ensure that all of the information in this book is accurate.

Due to differing conditions, tools, and individual skills, the
publisher cannot be responsible for any injuries, losses, and/or
other damage which may result from the use of the information
in this book.

Library of Congress Cataloging-in-Publication Data Available

10 9 8 7 6 5 4 3 2 1

Published by Sterling Publishing Co., Inc.
387 Park Avenue South, New York, NY 10016
© 2004 by Brad Mee
Distributed in Canada by Sterling Publishing
% Canadian Manda Group, One Atlantic Avenue, Suite 105
Toronto, Ontario, Canada M6K 3E7
Distributed in Great Britain by Chrysalis Books Group PLC,
The Chrysalis Building, Bramley Road, London W10 6SP, England
Distributed in Australia by Capricorn Link (Australia) Pty. Ltd.
P.O. Box 704, Windsor, NSW 2756, Australia
Printed in China
All Rights Reserved

Sterling ISBN 1-4027-0919-6

CONTENTS

INTRODUCTION

The interior of the home has always been a haven for personalized design. Everything from the finish on the walls to the placement of the final accessory reflects the style and taste of the home owner through its distinctive detail. Today, the home has burst out of its shell, opening onto the landscape. The home's outdoor living spaces—porches, verandas, decks, patios, and more—have become an extension of the interior, literally and decoratively tying them to the outlying gardens and grounds. And just like the interior rooms, these outdoor sanctuaries call upon detail to infuse them with unmistakable charm and character.

The secret to designing and decorating a vibrant and unique outdoor living space is treating it as you would treat one indoors. After all, the garden is part of the home and deserves the same attention to detail as do any of the home's interior spaces. From a practical standpoint, if one has decorating experience and views outdoor spaces like those indoors, the creative process will seem more familiar and come more naturally.

The first step to creating a beautiful outdoor room is determining its overall style. This is an important decision because the chosen style will influence all future design choices you make. Do you like a dynamic modern or Mediterranean look, or do you prefer the understated beauty of Zen or formal design? Be imaginative and selective. Your chosen style should be one you love and an expression of your personality. It should also complement the design of the existing home and landscape so that the entire property blends together with ease. Once the style is determined, detail steps in and the fun begins.

Where do you find detail in the outdoor room? It is simple—anywhere interest and eye-catching character exists, there is detail. It first touches the bones of the space—floors, walls, ceilings—the structural surfaces that frame the room. Similar to inside the home, outdoor surface detail may take such forms as stone, wood, or concrete. On the other hand, it could just as easily be a dense hedge, creeping ground cover, or a leafy overhead branch of a shade tree. The garden offers wonderful options. Furniture, accessories, and lighting, similar to those indoors, also provide distinctive detail that plays an important part in defining the style of the outdoor room. Special accents and fixtures can also add delicious flavor outdoors. In the garden, flowing fountains, flaming fireplaces, and arching arbors are among countless features that add character and charm while enhancing outdoor living.

Living is what the outdoor room is about. What activities do you envision in your open-air retreat? Dining, entertaining, playing, relaxing? The way you spend time in a space should influence the way it is designed. A quiet patio among serene gardens, a splashy pool under the sun, a welcoming conversation space surrounding a firepit, all reflect a way of living that brings purpose and life to the garden.

As you meander through the following pages, you will discover endless ideas to help you create your own one-of-a-kind outdoor living space. And like a stroll through a wandering garden, there are many stops along the way. There are examples of stunning surfaces, wonderful water and fire features, fantastic furnishings, and alluring accents designed to inspire and delight all who see them. Harvest the ideas you like, give them your own special touch, and spread them throughout your outdoor room. The result will be an oasis overflowing with your unique character and personal style.

STYLE

There is no better place to nurture your own sense of style than in the outdoor living areas of your home. Your patios, porches, gardens, and neighboring landscape are among the home's open-air "stages" welcoming theatrical settings and imaginative displays. Uniquely detailed floors, walls, and even ceilings act as backdrops to stunning water features, fashionable furnishings, distinctive accessories, and other dramatic elements. Together, they can create a bold and distinctive outdoor "roomscape" that reflects your personal style.

How do you define your own unique style? How does it color your ideal landscape? Do you envision a calm and serene setting with Zenlike order and natural understated elements? Perhaps you prefer a bold contemporary space with abstract yard-art, architectural vegetation, and sculpture-like furnishings. On the other hand, you may dream of a Mediterranean getaway overgrown with brightly colored flowers planted against a backdrop of sun-soaked stone, terracotta, and sparkling water. Whatever style you prefer, each has specific and identifiable elements that come together to create its individualistic look and feel. The goal is to determine your version of the perfect outdoor living space and to select the background and decorative features that bring it to life in the imaginative gardens of your home.

Through the ages, man has always used the landscape to make a statement of artful expression. Developing in medieval times and flourishing during and after the Renaissance, the formal garden became a unique style defined by symmetry and refined design. The geometrically bordered cloisters of European monasteries, the linear paths and topiaried plantings of Versailles, the tamed and statue-rich hillsides of Florence's Boboli gardens, all pay tribute

FORMAL

to this classic style. From their beauty, it is easy to become inspired and to develop ideas for one's own personal version of the classic garden and outdoor living area. Often thought of as highbrow and grand, the formal look translates wonderfully in today's home landscaping. Because these timeless gardens and outdoor rooms are best suited for enclosed areas, they are ideal for walled urban spaces and contained yards. If a landscape is vast, walls and hedges are instrumental in dividing the area into a number of smaller, roomlike settings fitting for formal's orderly style. Clipped hedges, stone benches, reflecting ponds, and linear plantings are among the many elements that combine to create formal outdoor roomscapes that are loved for their tranquility and controlled beauty.

Classic and timeless, the formally styled outdoor space has a restrained yet relaxing beauty. Its sense of order excludes anything distracting or off balance. It is highly symmetrical. To create a formally styled space, begin with a well-defined zone in the yard. Frame it with walls or trimmed hedges that act to enclose and define the area. Within the interior of the space there may be smaller secondary areas. Perhaps one will house an iron table and chairs, another a stone fountain, and another a parterre comprised of flowers and herbs planted in compartmentalized areas bordered by low-clipped boxwoods. Keep the walkways of the space and the overall landscape straight and angular. Any curves should be perfectly shaped to maintain a predictable and calming ambience—meandering paths are out of place here. To decorate a formally styled outdoor room, treat it as you would a traditionally fashioned interior space. Use classically styled furnishings—decorative wrought iron, carved stone, wood pieces with timeless lines. Use ageless accessories, such as ornate stone urns or iron wall sconces, in pairs and symmetrically placed. Just as indoors, the details of shape, proportion, and positioning are very important. Plantings and accent pieces should be appropriately sized for the room. Oftentimes topiaried trees and bushes are included as living sculpture. Classic stone or cast-concrete statues are used to add weight and antiquity to the room. Surfaces may include walls of ivy-covered brick, age-old stone, or dense foliage paired with crushed granite, brick, or stone floors. Most importantly, the surfaces should be plain or feature a uniform pattern. Abstract and jarring visuals are out of place in a formally styled outdoor room. This holds true for everything from walls to water features, accessories to accent pieces. The key is to keep the detail balanced, classic, and calm.

PAGE 12
Elegant statuary joins a pond filled with iris and water lilies to create a timeless and tranquil water feature in the yard.

PAGE 13
Low-clipped hedges, classically shaped planters, and a symmetrical placement of paths and furniture infuse this evergreen garden with formal style.

LEFT
Classic architecture becomes the perfect backdrop for a formal garden filled with stately topiaries, low stone walls, and orderly brick pathways, creating an irresistible setting for dining and entertaining.

ABOVE
Disciplined layers of tailored hedges, stone walkways, and sentrylike topiaried yew obelisks frame an elegant garden that defines the harmonious and restrained nature of formal design.

Bright sun-filled skies touching clay-colored earth; adobe, territorial, and hacienda-style homes embraced by broad patios, covered verandas, and walled courtyards—the desert is an open landscape that's a natural for outdoor living. Desert style invites a casual and relaxed lifestyle

DESERT

reflected by its homes, inside and out. The landscape rejects formality, choosing instead a free-form unstructured design. Outdoor desert spaces favor the use of slumped adobe walls paired with flagstone, aggregate stone, and saltillo floors. Overhead latilla screens also frame outdoor living with the desert's natural materials. The tribute continues with weathered pine chests, built-in "banco" benches, and traditional equipale chairs that surround beehive and chimenea fireplaces ablaze with crackling mesquite and piñon pine. Canterra-stone fountains, terra-cotta pots, and whimsical accessories fill the space while native cacti and succulents perform as living sculpture in the dynamic desert-style outdoor room.

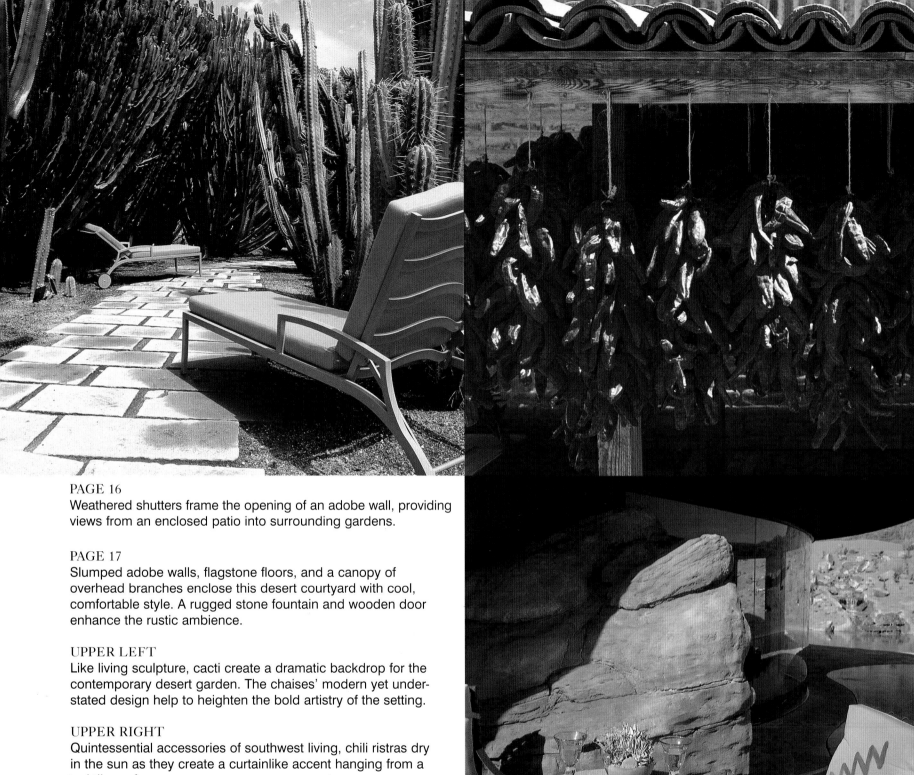

PAGE 16
Weathered shutters frame the opening of an adobe wall, providing views from an enclosed patio into surrounding gardens.

PAGE 17
Slumped adobe walls, flagstone floors, and a canopy of overhead branches enclose this desert courtyard with cool, comfortable style. A rugged stone fountain and wooden door enhance the rustic ambience.

UPPER LEFT
Like living sculpture, cacti create a dramatic backdrop for the contemporary desert garden. The chaises' modern yet under-stated design help to heighten the bold artistry of the setting.

UPPER RIGHT
Quintessential accessories of southwest living, chili ristras dry in the sun as they create a curtainlike accent hanging from a red tile roof.

LOWER RIGHT
Fluid architecture, native stone, and a sparkling pool combine comfortably in this stunning desert oasis. The home's large overhangs cool its interiors and generously provide shade for its multiple patio areas.

18

Desert-style gardens and outdoor rooms are best suited for hot dry climates where they reflect the character of the land. Far from barren, the desert is rich with stunning style. Native plant materials are only the beginning of the ways to decorate the arid garden landscape and outdoor room. Other elements include everything from weathered wooden gates and talevera pottery to scored concrete and contemporary architecture. Sun-washed colors and sparkling pools as well as stone-capped adobe walls and forever-brilliant bougainvillaea also enhance outdoor desert style.

RIGHT
Modern architecture and dramatic details have a permanent place in desert design. The grid pattern of this courtyard's stone ceiling repeats in the stone floor and iron chair backs. An eggplant-colored wall acts as a brilliant backdrop for an artlike presentation of cacti. A rounded, rugged stone water feature contrasts with the smooth surfaces and hard angles found throughout the space.

Stone, water, and foliage—three natural elements that come together to create Zen-style gardens. Although the harmonious nature of Zen outdoor spaces is much in vogue today, this distinctive style is hardly new. Buddhist monks actually created the first Zen gardens a thousand years ago as sites for meditation. Today, home owners across the globe draw upon the natural ingredients and design philosophy of the original Zen gardens to create tranquil contemplative retreats in their own yards. Here, visitors are at one with nature and surrounded by balanced and rhythmic placement of earth-borne elements. Stone is essential and used in many ways. Architecturally, large stones are strategically placed in odd numbers among beds of crushed gravel to create focal points representing mountains, hills, and islands.

ZEN

Ornamental stone pavers make walkways and bridges that provide access and visual direction to the property. Water—the source of life—takes form in placid pools, gurgling streams, and wondrous waterfalls that enhance the garden's sights and sounds. Finally, a constrained use of plant materials lends structure, color, and texture to the soulful Zen retreat. From shaped junipers to delicate Japanese maples and stone-covering mosses, carefully chosen and positioned plants complete the stylish and spiritual setting.

Look to nature when incorporating the beauty and serenity of Zen style into your outdoor living area. Simplicity and authenticity are key. Choose organic elements—native stone, naturally finished woods, orderly plantings. Remember that clutter and excitement are out of place here; keep the composition of the space balanced and clean. This holds true for everything from the patterns of raked gravel and the rhythmic placement of stone paths to the positioning of plant materials and the arrangement of furniture and accessories. Avoid kitschy or dramatic accent pieces and rely instead on traditional lanterns, spirit houses, bamboo wind chimes, and bridges to lend flavor and focal points to the restorative and relaxing retreat. In the Zen garden, views are thoughtfully framed with walls, screens, and plants. Wood decking and paneling, bamboo trellises, and pebbles and gravel create surface interest. Of course, there is water. Anything from a stone bowl of water to a reflective stream flowing over glistening moss-covered rock will enhance the harmonious nature of the space.

PAGE 20
Enormous stepping-stones lead from a tranquil pond while a trickle of water flows through a bamboo fixture into a purification stone, creating a secondary water feature in the space.

PAGE 21
Framing the view of an outdoor living area is important in a Zen-style space.

UPPER RIGHT
Woven modern furniture can make a bold statement in an otherwise tranquil Zen-style space.

LOWER RIGHT
Even a minute stone and water feature can help define the spiritual style of the Zen garden.

OPPOSITE
A carved-stone spirit house creates a strong focal point for outdoor Asian design.

OPPOSITE UPPER RIGHT
A pool of raked gravel represents a contemplative body of water where there is none.

OPPOSITE LOWER RIGHT
The still, reflective surface of water turns this pool into a poetic focal point.

Ask anyone about the perfect outdoor living space and chances are they will describe the heady beauty of the Mediterranean garden. After all, what's not to love? Sun-heated walls of rugged stone and mellow ochre-colored plaster acting as backdrops to painted

MEDITERRANEAN

shutters, iron gates, and hand-painted tile. Crushed gravel, warm clay tile, and a pattern-play of rough stone play underfoot as plantings of fig, olive, orange, and Cyprus trees grow skyward. Vine-covered arbors, shady loggias, and red tile roofs provide respite from the heat of the day, while tables of wrought iron, dark timber, and rugged stone are surrounded by casual wood, cane, or iron chairs—perfect for informal al fresco dining. Terra-cotta pots overflowing with trailing geraniums, shaped boxwood, and aromatic herbs create mobile gardens and a riot of color for patios, terraces, and courtyards. Sparkling pools and cascading fountains prove irresistible as inviting focal points and cool retreats. Mediterranean garden living is vibrant yet leisurely, sensuous yet robust. It is also relaxed and the details that shape its design should reflect this.

Importing the magic of the Mediterranean garden into your outdoor living space is simple. Be bold in your choices and remember that the more natural the elements, the better. Stone should be rough, not polished, and wood is best when worn and weathered. Tile may be chipped and furnishing's layers of paint left peeling. This is all part of the charm. Accessories, such as glazed terra-cotta urns, hand-painted ceramics, and stone statuary, look their best when aged and antiqued. Remember, people have been basking in the beauty of Mediterranean gardens for centuries. The details and design of the outdoor room should reflect it.

PAGE 24
A stone archway frames a relaxing patio shaded from the hot afternoon sun. A window incorporated in the back wall enables visitors to enjoy the beautiful views of the outlying countryside.

PAGE 25
Handmade Italian terra-cotta pots planted with citrus are classic details for Mediterranean outdoor areas. Placed in rows, they form living walls that can define distinct spaces within the landscape.

ABOVE
Detail thrives in the Mediterranean garden. Rustic stone and frescoed wall treatments, a canopy of wisteria infused with starlike lighting fixtures, terra-cotta pots and wooden and stone benches, all add magnificent character to this Tuscan hillside retreat.

> A house though otherwise beautiful, yet if it hath no garden belonging to it,
> is more like a prison than a house.
>
> William Goles

ABOVE
The Mediterranean home invites multiple outdoor living spaces. Here, a terrace next to the home overlooks open-air and covered patios ideal for outdoor relaxation and entertaining. Rugged stone surface treatments unite the spaces visually, while successive stairways and steps lead visitors, and the eye, from one space to the next.

Today's home, indoors and out, is experiencing a movement toward simpler, cleaner, and highly expressive design. Modern architecture and landscape design reflect this trend. Influenced by a desire to edit excess and confusion from their lives, creators

MODERN

of modern gardens and outdoor living areas are replacing the traditional landscape's profusion of flowering gardens and decorative ornaments with fewer, yet more dynamic, statements of personal style. In the modern outdoor roomscape, the detail of every element is considered a way to add unique character to the area. Form, pattern, texture, and tone become emphasized on everything from walls and floors, to furnishings, water features, and abstract sculptures. These outdoor spaces borrow materials and architectural design from the home and incorporate them into the landscape. This creates a sense of continuity and clarity from indoors to out. An attention to simple shapes, clean lines, and an arresting use of common as well as unexpected materials characterizes the modern garden space. It is this "material interest" that replaces the visual strength of casual garden beds filled with perky perennials. Here, formed concrete constitutes walls, planters, and platforms featuring intriguing profiles, texture-rich finishes, and bold colors. Steel takes shape in posts, planks, and screens boasting anything from satinlike stainless or rusted finishes to others that are polished or painted. Aluminum, copper, zinc, and iron are also metals that lend themselves to imaginative use in the modern garden. Stone,

glass, and wood can be similarly exploited. They all become integrated into the surfaces, features, and furnishings of the area. More than an open-air extension of a home, the modern outdoor area is a work of art that surprises and seduces those fortunate enough to step into the stylish space.

Purity of form is characteristic of contemporary design and has a strong influence on the modern garden space. Here, ornate and flowery silhouettes are out of place. Instead, strong linear and geometric shapes and patterns create the individuality and interest of the area. This philosophy influences everything from flooring surfaces, walls, and planters to water features, furniture, and even the plantings. In fact, the modern outdoor living area is often a gallery-like space showcasing artistic displays of succulents, clipped topiaries, and strongly sculptural vegetation in imaginatively fabricated containers.

PAGE 28
The boundaries between interior and exterior spaces disappear as contemporary architecture, bold water features, and common surface materials create a live-in work of art.

PAGE 29
Water features play an important part of a modern home's outdoor living area. Their forms and finishes create focal points in the landscape, while reflecting bold architectural and lighting details.

UPPER RIGHT
Turn to the outdoor furniture of a modern-style home to add sculptural forms and unique finishes to the space. Keep comfort and function in mind as well.

LOWER RIGHT
Dramatic lighting re-creates the modern landscape, highlighting strong architectural features and living areas, while leaving less-prominent areas in shadows and darkness.

OPPOSITE
The modern landscape is an artistic expression of its creator. A cascade of water falls from a wall fountain and flows underfoot through a partially open trough in the floor. The clean, polished design of the furniture enhances rather than detracts from this brilliant water feature.

Some of the most memorable outdoor living spaces are also the most comforting. Whether a sleeping porch, a broad veranda, or a quiet backyard deck, their charm is derived from their casual demeanor and carefree appearance. Romantic, country, and cottage garden spaces, all represent relaxed styles that welcome visitors with meandering paths, overgrown flower beds,

COMFORTING

cozy furnishings, and heartwarming detail. They are a reflection of the home owner's informal lifestyle and lighthearted approach to design. This is not to say that the comforting outdoor room has no plan, it simply lacks hard-and-fast regimentation, rules, and directives. Any sharp edges of garden structures or architecture are eased with creeping vines and climbing roses. Furniture is softened with floral-patterned pillows and woven blankets, and landscapes are graced with serene ponds, ageless oak trees, and white picket fences. The comforting garden doesn't impress with grandeur or bold artistic statements, but rather with a familiarity and natural style that is peaceful and reassuring.

> Gardens and flowers have a way of bringing people together, drawing them from their homes.
>
> Clare Ansberry

The comforting outdoor room, more than any other, borrows detail from inside the home to create its heartfelt style. In many cases, it becomes an extension of a much loved and nurtured interior. Woven rugs dress wooden porch floors and covered brick patios, while baskets and dried flowers hang from overhead rafters. White wicker chairs, pine rockers, and cast-iron benches are brightened with lively fabric-covered toss pillows. Glassware, ceramics, and favored accessories combine to create lively displays on outdoor ledges, shelves, and tabletops. Even shaded table lamps are brought outdoors to lengthen the enjoyment of a summer's evening with their warm golden glow. Of course, outdoor fixtures and accessories such as gazing balls, tin watering cans, garden tools, and whimsical garden art have a place here as well.

PAGE 33
Unfettered by formality, this romantic brick patio is framed by a rustic pergola and filled with unmatched furnishings and accessories. Randomly placed pieces and weathered, unmatched surfaces create its relaxed soulful ambience.

LEFT
Comforting gardens resist hard solid walls, preferring instead soft hedges, rose-covered arbors, and lighthearted picket fences to divide and define their outdoor living areas.

OPPOSITE
The front porch creates the first impression of a comforting home. Relaxed furnishings, fresh fabrics, soft lighting, and pots of blooming flowers reflect the carefree, easy living that makes this the most versatile and treasured space.

When it comes to a beautifully designed outdoor "room," what surrounds it is just as important as what is inside of it. Its architectural boundaries—the floor underfoot, the ceiling above, the surrounding walls—define the physical dimension of the space as they frame its size and volume. They also help define the character and personality of the outdoor room with the colors, textures, and patterns of arresting materials. The unique qualities of surface treatments become the foundation of the outdoor room's overall look and an expression of a home owner's personal style and taste.

Outdoor surface options are many. Some people prefer a natural and understated treatment, like a pebble-strewn floor or leafy overhead canopy, while others take a highly stylized approach using elaborately patterned brick pads and latticework screens. The possibilities seem endless. Not only are surface treatments stylish statements of their own, they can also effect the space's other decorative elements, becoming the backdrop for the room's plantings, furnishings, and accents. A small fountain embedded in a roughly stuccoed wall, a loosely arranged flagstone floor set among creeping thyme, a framework of overhead beams covered in wisteria, all are examples of how surfaces join with other design elements to produce a wonderful effect. To successfully create the foundation of your own outdoor oasis, select surface materials that not only shape the look and feel you desire for the space, but also complement the style of the home and its landscape.

Close your eyes and imagine stepping out into a garden. Feel the dampness of a dewy lawn underfoot, the warmth of sunbaked brick, or the cool smoothness of ceramic tile. Now open your

FLOORS

eyes and look downward. The mottled coloration of natural pebbles, the grain of stained-wood decking, the pattern of moss growing between randomly laid stone, all welcome an appreciative gaze. These represent only a few of the ways to surface sensational outdoor floors. Of course, their beauty is more than skin deep. Flooring materials have a practical side as well. They provide transition from indoors to out and create secure, stable ground upon which to build an outdoor living area. They replace loose dirt, relieve areas of standing water, and are instrumental at shaping a multilevel roomscape. Overall, the floor of the outdoor room is the space's structural and stylish anchor and should be thoughtfully selected. A difficult choice? Perhaps the decision will come more easily as you wander barefoot among and open your eyes to the many material options available for your outdoor floor.

In the same way we labor over selecting just the right flooring inside a dwelling—hardwood, carpet, tile—we should be equally as thoughtful with our flooring choices outdoors. They, too, affect the practical and aesthetic enjoyment of the home. Outdoor flooring includes the surface upon which we create rooms, as well as the paths that connect them to surrounding areas. The flooring choices should be in keeping with the style of the home and garden, as well as with the intended use of the space. Sturdy durable materials are best for areas with high foot traffic such as main access paths, patios, terraces, and courtyards. Brick, stone, concrete, tile, and wood are all stable materials that can endure heavy use and look great doing it. Each has a look fitting for specific styles—for example, brick is ideal for traditional and country settings, saltillo tile for desert designs, and scored and stained concrete for modern spaces. Also keep in mind that specific materials can be uniquely arranged in elaborate patterns as well as combined with others to create distinctive, highly stylized flooring treatments for the rooms outdoors.

To me a lush carpet of pine needles or spongy grass is more welcome than the most luxurious Persian rug.

Helen Keller

PAGE 39
Adding color and texture, a round mosaic inlay creates the look and feel of an area rug centered on this private courtyard's tiled floor.

OPPOSITE
Stone is the perfect flooring foundation for natural-style settings. Herbs, like creeping thyme, can be planted between the stones so that their fragrance is released every time someone walks across the surface.

LEFT
Gravel offers a natural-looking, low-maintenance flooring option for outdoor rooms. Perfect when used in tranquil Mediterranean and Modern style spaces alike, a gravel "carpet" is ideal for outdoor paths and carefree dining areas.

Heaven is beneath our feet as well as over our heads.

Henry David Thoreau

Paving not only creates a hard surface upon which to establish a living area, it also provides an opportunity for personalized design. Just as inside the home, the pattern in which an outdoor flooring material is placed influences the look and feel of the space. Strong clean lines and established patterns are perfect for contemporary designs as well as disciplined traditional settings. On the other hand, a more random arrangement of materials complements the loose and casual setting of a country and desert dwelling, for example. Pattern can also be useful in directing the eye and movement in the space. Long linear arrangements draw the eye and foot traffic in the direction the pattern leads, while circular and centered patterns visually attract the eye into the core of the space.

ABOVE
More than just a solid surface upon which to walk, paving can be used like interior carpeting and floorings to add character to the outdoor room. Dramatically designed patterns, created from modular pavers of various shades, enliven a pool and patio area (left). An imaginative use of aggregate stone, brick, and hand-painted tile becomes the focal point of a courtyard's floor (center). Tile of varied sizes, shapes, and shades offers the opportunity to create the look of an inlaid area rug on the underfoot surface of outdoor living spaces (right).

OPPOSITE
Timber decking takes on a new life when a black-and-white "area rug" is painted across its surface. The treatment adds eye-catching detail and defines the dining area of the deck.

PAGES 44–45
Patterned flooring effectively breaks up the space of a large outdoor area. Like lily pads on a pond's surface, large circular medallions float across the brick-stacked pattern of this spacious courtyard. The treatment creates movement and interest across the surface.

Paths are multitalented. They direct the eye and guide physical movement throughout the landscape, providing access to various living spaces in the yard. Their sinuous curves, sharp corners, and changes of elevation create interest and intrigue. Furthermore, they offer wonderful opportunities to detail the garden with the color, texture, and distinctive patterns of the materials that pave them.

OPPOSITE

A path of indigenous stones loosely laid within a garden creates the natural look of a dried-up streambed (upper left). Dark natural stones provide access to an upper patio and transition into the woodsy landscape that surrounds them (lower left). The risers on steps provide a canvas upon which to express a garden's intended style. Hand-painted Mexican tiles and Spanish motifs add color to an outdoor breezeway (lower right).

LOWER AND RIGHT

Boldly creative, cylindrical stepping stones provide access to the entry of a modern desert home. Taller pillars add height and drama (lower left). The step risers of this brick walkway are simply bricks set on end. The aged brick's casual pattern is perfectly suited to the traditional home's free-flowing landscape of wildflowers (lower right). Crushed gravel has carpeted garden paths for centuries. An inset border helps define the path and keeps it from encroaching on the flower beds (right).

If trying to determine how to create a stylish outdoor living space has you climbing the walls, you may have already discovered the answer. After all, walls represent one of the most important elements used to divide a landscape into distinctive, well-defined areas. In the garden, the term "wall" is loosely defined. It may be a traditional brick-and-mortar enclosure, but just as easily may be a robust hedge, a cast-iron fence, or a lattice screen covered with ivy. If it is vertical and plays a part in dividing the property and defining its architecture, it is a wall. Whatever its

WALLS

form, a wall not only helps delineate roomlike outdoor spaces, it also provides a sense of privacy and shelter for everything it encloses. Additionally, walls provide enormous opportunity to enrich an outdoor space with unique detail overflowing with character and style.

PAGE 48
An antique iron grate maintains the security of this courtyard while adding both character and a view of the surrounding landscape.

PAGE 49
The height, dimensions, and surface treatment of adjoining garden walls strongly influence the style of this space. A low, unassuming stucco wall contrasts with a tall neighboring stone wall while aggregate inlaid floors "up" the area's drama.

RIGHT
An adobe-block wall with slumped-mud "relief" single-handedly defines this desert courtyard's character.

OPPOSITE
A ringtoss of grapevine wreaths decorate barn wood-covered walls with texture and comfortable country charm.

Walls not only define the boundaries of an outdoor room, they also offer themselves as distinctive and decorative treatments that personalize the garden space. Look at the wall as a way to infuse your exterior living space with color, texture, and delicious detail. Consider enlisting the rich pattern-play of inlaid tile, brick, or stone. Display images and motifs with painted murals, tiles, and intricately styled mosaics. Inset a window-like opening or enclose panels of ornately scrolled wrought iron, or weathered wooden shutters to frame a view. Train climbing vines or espaliered fruit trees to grow on its surface and consider installing a wall fountain for a dramatic effect. The possibilities are only limited by your imagination.

A garden must be
looked unto
and dressed,
as the body.

George Herbert

RIGHT
A vine-covered arbor and
hand-forged iron gate create
an intriguing entry from a
lush courtyard into a yet-to-
be-discovered garden.

OPPOSITE
In outdoor spaces, a door
can do more than provide
security. Its unique form,
finish, and placement can
make it a primary decorative
feature for any distinctively
designed courtyard, patio,
or garden.

Like sentries, doors and gates guard a home while welcoming guests to the garden and introducing them to the special places within. Solid doors suggest protection and guard the home from unwanted intrusion. Because they are often the focal point for a courtyard or garden entrance, their design is an important contributor to the aesthetic beauty of the landscape. Make certain they complement rather than compete with the design and architecture of the home. Iron gates can also provide security as well as an interesting partition in a wall. Their unique detail is eye-catching yet seems to vanish as the gates disappear into the view of outlying gardens yet to be discovered.

"Wallcoverings" in the garden are just as important as those used indoors and deserve equal consideration in their selection. A wall treatment's color, texture, and pattern-play can set the tone of the entire outdoor room. When deciding on a surface element, be creative and thoughtful of neighboring architecture and design details. Also be mindful of its physical effect upon the space. Whether stone, wood, plastered concrete, brick, tile, or fencing interwoven with thriving vines, a surface treatment can influence the temperature, sound, and, of course, visual experience of the area it encloses. For example dark solid walls attract and retain heat, whereas lightly colored and glossy surfaces are better at reflecting it. Screens of lattice and vegetation also reduce heat in the area and allow air as well as noise to flow more easily into its space.

RIGHT
Deeply colored and crumbling, aged-plaster walls lend authenticity and irresistible charm to a Mediterranean style courtyard.

CENTER RIGHT
Haute and hip, these blue mosaic walls dress this poolside patio with fresh style and distinctive detail. A round "porthole" window accessorizes the surface dramatically.

FAR RIGHT
Like a mouthful of misaligned teeth, the slats of this fence playfully overlap as they imaginatively accent the theatrical entry of this stacked-stone home.

If you are searching for a way to add distinctive detail and bold character to your outdoor living space, things are looking up. The ceiling offers one of the most effective yet overlooked ways to cover the space with

CEILINGS

undeniable style. Consider the options—gridlike pergolas, canvas awning architectural overhangs, and broad umbrellas are just a few of the many ways to provide shelter from the elements while "capping" the space with stylish detail. When designing your room's overhead treatment, be imaginative. The stylistic possibilities are infinite. Of course, don't forget about the most obvious choice; the canopy of a shade tree creates a soulful ceiling of light and shadow that is timeless and forever changing.

Outdoor ceilings combine form and function in a beautiful way. Providing protection from hot sunlight, wind, and rain, solid ceilings act as barriers to the elements. They can be shaped and styled from endless materials and enhance the design-quotient of the space. Overhead screens of woven lattice and frameworks of beams are as equally decorative but offer less defense from nature. Even so, they encourage light and weather to break through in patterns that decoratively play on the floors and walls of the outdoor room.

PAGES 56–57
Hovering above this vista-rich veranda, an open timber-framed ceiling treatment defines the style and dimensions of the broad outdoor living area. Its dramatic overhead pattern repeats in shadows on the floor below.

LEFT
Designed to define rather than shelter the space of this contemporarily styled patio, the engineered canopy of white beams is held aloft with colorful supports and surprising columns with Doriclike capitals.

OPPOSITE
Sculpted cross-vaulted ceilings have characterized dramatic architecture for centuries. This ceiling detail joins multiple archways to help divide the expansive loggia into separate seating and entertaining areas. It also creates the decidedly Italian style of the space.

The overhead treatments of a garden frame the space, helping to define its living area as well as its overall style.

OPPOSITE
In this desert setting where nature takes precedence, rough-hewn logs simply frame rather than protect outdoor living areas. They help create the illusion of open-air "rooms" venturing from the home into the landscape. Other more "traditional" patios are sheltered by large overhangs and semienclosed spaces.

LOWER LEFT
Raise a large market umbrella, and an outdoor living space suddenly takes shape. Umbrellas detail a garden with color, architecture, and scale. Unlike fixed ceiling features, they can provide any area of the landscape with a mobile form of protection from blazing sun or drizzling rain.

UPPER LEFT AND LOWER RIGHT
Though not protective, overhead grids of wood and metal, can enhance outdoor rooms of endless styles. They help to define the exterior style of a home, delineate the dimensions of the outdoor room, and add a sense of coziness to a space by visually enclosing it from above.

Porches, verandas, and covered patios, all enjoy the same overhead protection as rooms indoors. And just like their interior counterparts, these spaces deserve to have the same detail-oriented attention paid to their ceiling treatments. Color and texture can add interest, while soaring beams, paneling, sculpted contours, and the unusual applications of varied materials can add bold architectural statements.

RIGHT
A lofty beamed ceiling shapes the character and dimensions of this Spanish style patio. An iron chandelier hangs like jewelry from the ceiling's main beam, enhancing the bold style of the space.

OPPOSITE
By painting the ceiling of this serene veranda blue, the semi-darkened overhead surface visually drops, making the overall space feel cozier and more comfortable. On the other hand, the ceiling's glossy finish reflects light, giving it dimension and visually raising it, keeping it from seeming to "drop" too low. This counterbalancing effect is tranquil and soothing.

ELEMENTS

Today's high-style outdoor living space is more than an extraneous room beyond a home's interior. It's a setting alive with detail that transforms a lackluster landscape into a sanctuary in which to retreat, relax, and revitalize. Three of the most celebrated elements that help create a personal outdoor oasis are water features, fireplaces, and uniquely designed garden structures. Each performs a unique magic upon the space, coloring it with character that reflects the personality and style of the home owner. Some people prefer the subtlety of a trickling fountain, small firepit, and distant arbor, while others like a splashy waterfall pool, a roaring fireplace, and a dramatic pergola. Of course, each of these elements performs beyond its beauty in the space. Water features provide movement, architecture, and alluring sounds outdoors. Fireplaces offer warmth as well as a sense of indoor living under the stars. Of course, unique garden structures create stylish and shady destinations within a yard. They all serve as focal points in the outdoor living space, color it with character, and draw an appreciative eye to their unique design and detail.

Like a wand-wielding wizard, water in the garden casts its spell on everyone who sees or hears it. Its sparkling surface, mesmerizing movement, and soulful sounds enchant even the most casual visitor. Depending on the style of feature used, water has the ability to sooth, inspire, and excite with its presence. A still pond or burbling fountain can imbue a courtyard with calmness, just as a rushing waterfall or daring pool can deliver drama to an adjoining patio or deck. Water features are frequently the focal point of a yard or outdoor room. They draw the eye to their stylish forms and to the sparkling and reflective waters they contain. Water features create a mood

WATER

with their sounds alone—the splash of a waterfall, the trickling of a fountain, the rush of a stream—as they cover and disguise undesirable noises from neighboring homes and streets. Undoubtedly water's most impressive trick is its ability to make a space overflow with personality and unforgettable style.

As the garden has developed into the home's open-air retreat, water features have become an integral part of the landscape and outdoor living area. Whatever their form, from pools and brooks to ponds and fountains, they attract activity, reflect sparkling sunlight, and eye-catching design into the space. The style of the water feature, like other elements of the well-planned landscape, should fit the architecture and design of the home and gardens. Its size and scale must also be appropriate for the property. For instance, geometric pools, stone statuary, and classic wall fountains fashioned from refined materials complement a formal garden room and landscape. On the other hand, free-form ponds, rock-framed waterfalls, and dark-bottomed pools are better suited for the natural landscapes of casual mountain, desert, and country settings. When appropriately and imaginatively designed, the water feature—large or small—adds immeasurable character and charm to the outdoor living area.

PAGE 67
Multiple water features can work well together. Integrated into the architecture of the home, this sparkling pool draws upon classically designed fountains to add character and sound to the landscape.

LEFT
A profusion of waterside plantings and lush gardens are the backdrop for this enticing multilevel backyard pond. Water spills from a wall fountain and a leaf-covered basin, filling the entire garden with the music of splashing water and the nature it attracts.

RIGHT
In keeping with its natural surroundings, a ledge is paved with stone and serves as a small patio from which to enjoy the beauty of a flowing stream.

How often it is that a garden, beautiful though it may be, will seem sad and dreary and lacking in one of its most gracious features, if it has no water.

Pierre Husson

Fountains serve as alluring focal points that elevate the style of the garden. Whether it is splashing water falling from bowl-to-bowl, the gentle burbling of an overfilled vessel, or the trickling of drops from a bamboo spout, be conscious of the sound a fountain creates. Make certain that it enhances rather than overwhelms the space in which the fountain is placed.

Gone are the days of the "cement pond" positioned squarely in the middle of the yard, dominating the garden and surrounding landscape. Yesterday's pool was set away from the home and acted as a separate destination and entity. Today, these isolated pools and ponds have been replaced with water accents that are fully integrated into the outdoor architecture and living areas. What's more, these high-style features often include more than one type of waterworks, combining pools with fountains, ponds with waterfalls, and brooks with basins. Dramatic or restrained, these features conjoin an artful display of architecture, nature, water, and personal style.

UPPER RIGHT
A spout set into a stone lion-head starts the chain of spilling water that flows from two half bowls into a dark-bottomed pool. Each additional level of falling water increases the intrigue of this majestic feature and the sounds it brings to the poolside area.

LOWER RIGHT
Steps not only provide access to the raised deck of this pool, but they also make a bold architectural statement for this contemporary, angular water feature.

OPPOSITE
With indigenous stone and dark underwater surface, a pool appears natural in open settings like that of this stunning desert abode.

Roasting marshmallows over an open flame, gathering with friends around a roaring campfire, dining al fresco among burning candles—the

FIREPLACES

power to enhance the outdoor living experience has always been magical. Its dancing flames, smoky aroma, and relaxing heat have made fire a must-have for fine living under the stars. Why not incorporate fire into your outdoor living space? There are many imaginative ways to do this. Elaborate stone fireplaces, shouldered with broad mantles and hearty hearths make awe-inspiring architectural elements that decoratively anchor

outdoor rooms and perform as their main focal points. Ground-level or raised firepits invite admirers to gather around, while small mobile fire "bowls" that can be moved from spot to spot provide flexibility and delightful detail in the garden. Whatever form the fire feature takes, it can turn up the heat on dramatic design as it chases away the cool of the night and lengthens the season for living outdoors.

To determine the style of an outdoor fireplace as well as its position in the landscape, consider its purpose and the activities it will enhance. As a focal point, fire is most dynamic when placed near water. The contrast of these two elements and the reflection of flames on a pool's surface are stunning. In this setting, raised firepits and bowls are ideal as they expose as much flame to the water's surface as possible. On the other hand, if the purpose for the fireplace is to provide warmth and to anchor a conversation area, the fireplace should feature a raised firebox, be close to the home, and cozy-up to the sitting area around it. When positioned adjacent to the home, they support a secondary living area that is easily reached and can be enjoyed throughout the seasons.

PAGE 75
The inherent natural beauty of stone adds to the drama of this raised firepit and the sentrylike water features behind it. It is the focal point of the patio and, when not "fired-up," it serves as a round bench from which to enjoy the surrounding landscape.

OPPOSITE LEFT
A small gas-fed firepit extending from an outdoor wall enhances the view from the nearby master bedroom, while providing warmth for the relaxed patio on a chilly desert night.

OPPOSITE RIGHT
A favorite for of outdoor nighttime living, the portable steel firepit creates magical ambience on any small patio, poolside deck, or dark corner of a leafy garden.

LEFT
Built into the corner of a wrap-around covered porch, this rock-faced fireplace can be enjoyable throughout the year. Its raised firebox makes the blazing logs visible from across the landscape and creates a convivial focal point for friends and family.

PAGE 78
A jagged, stacked-rock fireplace dramatically divides a large covered patio into separate living areas. Its crackling fire, visible from either side of the fireplace, and adjacent crescent-shaped banco seating offer a comfortable place to enjoy the fire's warmth and nighttime views.

PAGE 79
Firepits create irresistible destinations in the landscape. Place one far into the yard or on a patio and it will draw visitors like moths to a flame.

Few can resist the allure of a beautifully designed outdoor structure. Whether it is a roomlike gazebo, a wandering pergola, or a simple rose-covered arbor shaded with fragrant blooms, these idyllic structures infuse a landscape with beauty and

STRUCTURES

architectural strength and charm. Visually, garden structures are some of the most effective focal points for a landscape as they draw the eye to their distinctive forms and finishes—walls of lattice, passages of shapely arches, walkways of beamed canopies. At the same time the features attract decorative detail, they can also divert the eye from less appealing elements elsewhere on the property. Built close to the home, they often serve as a transition from the house to the patio, pool, or garden. Placed well into the recesses of the landscape, they add depth, dimension, and an alluring destination to venture out and visit.

PAGE 80
An enclosed gazebo serves garden visitors throughout the year as they commune with the garden's nature even during inclement weather. An attached brick patio further extends the outdoor living hosted by this handsome structure.

PAGE 81
A garden gate becomes more than just a pass-through when ornate ironwork adds a decorative garden archway.

LEFT
This grand, open-air gazebo brings commanding architecture to the surrounding landscape. Its classic styling lends a statement of formality to the garden's otherwise natural design.

LOWER LEFT
Strategically placed, gazebos can be the favorite spot in the yard from which to enjoy the aroma of fragrant roses, the sounds of falling water, and the views of a well-tended garden.

LOWER RIGHT
In an open landscape, a gazebo can instantly create an outdoor garden room in which to relax and dine. Add climbing vines, accent lighting, and comfortable furnishing, and the result is a favored getaway in the yard.

Garden structures are like magical hideaways that act as shaded retreats within a yard. They create focal points and add to the architecture of the garden. Some are large and substantial, while others are less formidable but equally as charming. Gazebos, meaning gazing out, are wonderful open-air abodes that can be designed and detailed like small living areas secondary to the patios, terraces, and decks of the home. Their furnishings and accessories set the tone and activities of the gazebo, providing a place to dine, relax, or daydream. These furnishings should be able to stand up to weather or be easily moved. Arbors and pergolas are also favored getaways in the garden, but perform more as passageways than destinations. They mark magical transitions from one area of a garden into another. Built-in benches can, however, turn a moment strolling through these structures into leisure time spent seated under rose-covered arches and crisscross beamwork.

RIGHT
Tucked away in the corner of the comforting garden, this charming pavilion provides a private retreat away from the hustle and bustle of the home.

ACCENTS

The surfaces are set, the fixed elements are established, and now it is time to accent the space with furniture, accessories, and lighting. Although the focus is on the completion of an outdoor living space, it could just as easily be the finalization of an interior room. Indoors or out, distinctively designed and functional living areas require finishing accents. This is the secret to completing a wonderfully detailed outdoor living space—think of it as you would one indoors. Fill a garden with furniture that makes your time spent comfortable and pleasurable. Select pieces that accommodate whatever activities you enjoy—cooking, dining, reading, relaxing, entertaining. The same holds true of accessories. Select those that make you happy and enhance the style you have chosen for the yard. Whether an accessory is a functional piece such as a birdbath, or purely decorative like a gazing ball, it can add character to the outdoor living area and punctuate it with your personal style. Of course, without lighting, the hours spent enjoying the outdoor room would be limited to those brightened by the sun. With the addition of well-chosen lighting, a garden can take on a second life and be enjoyed long into the night. Finally, when accenting your garden, think of your home's interior. Many furnishings that make a room come to life indoors can also be used in your living area under the stars—it just takes a bit of daring and imagination.

Think of some of the most enjoyable times spent in an outdoor living area and it is likely they involve furniture. Sunning on a luxurious chaise,

FURNITURE

dining at a table surrounded by friends, napping in a wonderful woven hammock. . . all are among moments cherished. These are also the times when garden furniture performs at its best. It not only becomes part of the experience of life beyond a home's interior, it actually enhances it. Furniture serves a function providing a place to rest, eat, and entertain. In addition, today's outdoor furniture performs double duty as it acts as high-style sculpture in the outdoor space. Designers and manufacturers alike have morphed the clunky, passionless silhouettes of yesterday's furniture into head-turning designs that turn the ho-hum garden space into an oasis of comfort and stunning style.

Forget about yesterday's weather-worn pine picnic table and folding aluminum chairs with crisscrossing plastic straps. Today's outdoor furniture has evolved from the practical predictables of the past into eye-catching pieces with enough style and substance to compete with its trendsetting indoor counterparts. In fact, many of the furniture pieces used outdoors today can work double duty when also used indoors. The key to selecting the right furniture for your outdoor space is to first establish its purpose and how much use it will receive. Next determine the amount and type of exposure to the elements it will experience. These points not only help clarify the type of pieces needed, from dining and lounging to cooking and entertaining, but also the type of materials best suited for the construction of the furnishings. For example, cast iron is long-lasting, teak ages beautifully when weathered, and stone is, of course, resilient and timeless. With practical considerations in hand, you can then turn to the aesthetics. Just like indoors, furniture in the garden should be in keeping with the style of the home. Its size and scale should be properly proportioned to the room. Of course, comfort is paramount; furniture should be a pleasure to use. Whether it is a lounge by the pool, a bench along a winding path, or a stool pulled up to an open-air bar, outdoor furniture should be beautiful to the eye, practical to use, and an irresistible place to rest and relax as you enjoy the great outdoors.

PAGE 87
Dreamlike in their beauty, a pair of contoured woven chaises is draped in canopies of sheer gauze. The resulting sculpted forms lend drama and indulgent comfort to the enchanting thatch-roofed veranda in which they are placed.

LEFT
Indoors and out, the furniture of a room—its color, shape, and material—is an expression of its owner's tastes and an influential part of the design scheme. Enlist the help of unique furnishings to color your garden space with distinctive detail.

OPPOSITE
Perfect for a morning's casual breakfast or a late-night chat in front of the fire, a circle of chairs is like a magnet, naturally drawing patio visitors to gather around and enjoy the garden in the company of friends and family.

Don't let the good look of today's garden furniture blind you to the functional needs of the outdoor living space. After all, any room, indoors or out, isn't enjoyable if it isn't equipped to function well. In most homes, the patios, porches, terraces, and decks multitask as places to not only sit and relax but also to cook, dine, and entertain. The best furniture for these spaces is that which accommodates these numerous activities—and does so with style. When selecting furniture to meet your needs, consider the number of guests you normally like to host; then determine the suitability of pieces by examining a table's size (with and without extension leaves), the number of accompanying chairs, and the seating capacity of neighboring benches, lounges, and chaises. This is critical for successful party giving. Also look for useful accent pieces like carts, chests, and side-tables that provide storage for cushions and supplies as well as surface space for preparing, serving, and dining al fresco.

OPPOSITE UPPER LEFT
A teak chest provides a stylish and easily accessible place to store cushions, pillows, and pool toys while protecting them from the elements when not in use.

OPPOSITE LOWER LEFT
Active outdoor rooms are home to impromptu parties and cozy, late-night dinners. Serving carts and trolleys can make entertaining easy by offering a mobile serving surface.

LEFT
Weather is a challenge to outdoor furniture. Teak is a wonderful hardwood that not only stands up to the elements, but becomes more beautiful as it weathers and ages naturally.

It is said that life's simplest pleasures are often the sweetest. This explains the allure of classically designed tree seats, garden benches, and Adirondack chairs. They add immeasurable charm to any landscape and beckon visitors of the garden to take a seat, if only for a moment, and enjoy the natural beauty that surrounds them.

ABOVE
Timelessly styled, this mobile bench provides a ready seat and classic charm anywhere it is placed in the garden.

OPPOSITE
There are few things as simply beautiful and inviting as a white tree seat encircling a broad-armed shade tree. Throughout the seasons, it furnishes a remote "room" framed by the open landscape and canopy of overhead branches.

One hour of thoughtful solitude may nerve the heart for days of conflict.

Percival

Never underestimate the power of a solitary piece of furniture. Its form, design, and detail can define the style of a space and the activity it intends. A lone hammock is an unmistakable invitation to lay back and leisurely count clouds overhead. A single bench along a garden's path, on the other hand, suggests a temporary seat at which to stop and enjoy the flowers before continuing on your way. Additionally, a patio chaise, luxuriously cushioned and paired with a convenient side table, offers itself to hours of reclining with a good book and a glass of lemonade. Regardless of the piece, when considering its placement, think about its decorative effect on the outdoor surroundings and the use it is intended to accommodate.

No well-designed space, indoors or out, is complete without accessories. They are the finishing touches, the special objects that give a room its own distinct style. Considering all the unique and colorful pieces in the garden and outdoor living areas, it may be difficult to determine which are actually considered accessories. After all, these features are not only decorative, but they are practical objects that bring character and color to the space.

ACCESSORIES

What items bring your garden to life? In most outdoor spaces, accessories are everywhere. Birdbaths, wreaths, statues, wind chimes, all attract the eye to their forms while reflecting the tastes of their owners. Likewise, urns, pots, pillows, and even watering cans help deepen the personality of a garden. Fun or functional, these contributory pieces are hard workers. They create focal points in the garden, add spots of structure and color, and create drama and rhythm as they lead the eye around the space. Country to classic, woodsy to whimsical, all outdoor styles benefit from the eye-catching ornamental objects.

Containers are favorite accessories that both serve and stylize the decorated garden. Aged stone urns and terra-cotta pots filled with trailing ivy and geraniums, galvanized buckets and wicker baskets planted with herbs and annuals, and even empty moss-lined baskets and old stoneware stacked in rows become functional art that brings carefree character to the space.

PAGE 96
A country cottage delights with a profusion of charming accessories. Entangled in creeping vines, bordered by a clipped hedge, and shadowed by a rustic wooden overhang, these cherished objects meld into the setting with ease and undeniable charm.

RIGHT
Nothing brings color and life to the garden room like flowering plants. But don't stop there—the containers that hold them can also brighten the space with unique character. Be creative and bold. After all, if a planter doesn't fit, it can always be moved or replaced.

Don't overlook the garden's working pieces when choosing accessories for outdoor spaces. Whether you select a weather vane, sundial, trellis, or even a collection of wash buckets, the forms and finishes of functional garden objects have a beauty and style all their own.

A house becomes a home when it is filled with items that are special to its owners. This is true indoors and out. Gardens and outdoor living spaces invite lively displays of favorite objects, cherished collectibles, and one-of-a-kind details. They are the perfect place to play up your personality as they welcome anything and everything that adds to their distinctive style.

OPPOSITE
Layers of accessories bring the flavor of the old west to this rustic mountain home. Vintage fabrics brighten weathered furniture, while potted plants add nature's charm. Indoor accents— shaded lamps, pillows, ceramics—infuse comfort while carved Indian statues and wagon wheels create boldly decisive finishing touches.

LEFT
Birdhouses have grown from practical, one-room studios for our feathered friends into popular architectural ornaments that capture the eye and imagination.

While the moon and stars may serve as nature's night-lights, it takes well-designed lighting to truly bring a garden to life after dark. At night, lighting washes the garden in layers—some subtle, others dramatic—re-creating the look and feel of the outside living area and making it a magical extension of those indoors. Lighting can actually transform the character of the garden as it highlights unique design, exaggerates detail, and becomes a guide leading the eye and venturesome visitors throughout the garden. Lighting also provides security and enhances nighttime activities in the outdoor living area. To determine how best to highlight the beauty of your landscape, predetermine how the space will be used and how you would like it to appear after dark. Provide task or service

LIGHTING

lighting for areas of activity—cooking, dining, and swimming for example. Select the architectural and landscape features you would like to emphasize and accent them with light. Illuminate walkways and meandering paths for safety and to create a rhythm in the darkened yard. Of course, use flickering candle flames, fire, and soft lamplight to infuse the outdoor living area with a relaxed and enchanting atmosphere.

The practice of flooding a night-time landscape has ended. Instead, minimal lighting is used to create pockets of interest and to enhance, rather than overwhelm, the outdoor living area. Up-lighting, down-lighting, and path lighting can accentuate trees and art, brighten walkways, and highlight a home's architectural strengths and brilliant water features. Of course, even simple treatments like a string of party lights, a group of burning candles, or a set of twinkling votives can add a festive feel to an otherwise dark and lifeless garden.

PAGE 104
Candlelight has immense power to create ambience. Positioning candles at different places and levels in a room creates pools of interest and illumination throughout.

PAGE 105
This home's interior becomes one with a well-lit landscape. The reflective property of the large pool magnifies the magic of lighting as well as the dynamic ceiling treatment of the interior living area.

OPPOSITE
Scattered votives and draped strings of lights instantly turn an enclosed patio into a festive and fun-filled spot to spend the evening.

LEFT
Embedded in this winding flagstone walkway, small lights guide visitors to the front door, while creating a stunning surface treatment underfoot. Discreet ground level lighting and a primary wall sconce illuminate the entry for practical purposes.

Water and nighttime lighting can pair with dramatic results. Underwater lighting can make an entire pool or fountain glow. Left dark, these same waters can become mirrorlike, reflecting and doubling the visual impact of neighboring landscape and architectural features accented with light. In addition, moving water from flowing streams, splashy fountains, and rushing waterfalls becomes animated with well-directed lighting. With each of these approaches, it is important that the lighting fixtures are concealed and their glare minimized. This way, the focus remains on the water and the reflection from the nearby garden and its details.

RIGHT
Expertly designed lighting brings this nighttime desert landscape to life. Throughout the property, lighting accentuates the natural rock, flowing waters, and casual living spaces. During the day the space is beautiful; but thanks to the lighting, it becomes equally as breathtaking at night.

In the right light, at the right time, everything is extraordinary.

Aaron Rose

Candles can make any setting special. Used in the garden, they create a romantic, magical mood. Lanterns can be used to protect candle flames from the elements and exaggerate their glow through the glass. They are perfect as accent pieces and used in rows along a pool's edge. Torches can also withstand a breeze and are a wonderful way to light a walkway or brighten a party's perimeter. In the still of the night, tapered and pillar candles can be used in groups to make bold statements of style as their naked flames dance in the darkness. Small votive candles scattered on an outdoor dining table or placed along the top of a wall create a twinkling light that is delicate and delightful.

Picture the perfect outdoor room and imagine the many ways you would use and enjoy its space. As you do, you will probably recognize that the most enjoyable outdoor living areas are not only beautifully detailed but are designed to operate effortlessly for those who use them. Most garden spaces are multi-functional. They offer a place for socializing, entertaining, and dining. They also have quiet areas in which to rest and relax. Furthermore, they blur the boundaries of, and create transition zones between, a home's high-style interior and the wilds of the open landscape beyond. When you design and detail your ideal outdoor living area, consider its purpose as well as its style. This is a practical step insures that it performs perfectly for you. Once you determine its functions, fill it with fixtures and features that will enhance your life outdoors.

PURPOSE

Outdoor entertaining has always been special. A Sunday morning brunch on an open-air patio, a romantic dinner on the terrace surrounded by candlelight, or an afternoon chat session among friends

ENTERTAIN

in the casual setting of a covered porch. These are just some examples of the times when outdoor living is at its best. There is something about dining and enjoying the company of guests al fresco that makes food taste better and friendships become closer. When entertaining outdoors, comfort is the key to creating wonderful times. Day or night, be mindful of the temperature. If necessary, provide supplemental

shading during hot days and stoke a fire or use space heaters during chilly evenings. Make certain there is adequate seating for all guests that is conveniently located and comfortably cushioned. Because dining is a favorite part of living under the stars, an outdoor room's furnishings, accessories, and lighting should enhance this experience. Design and detail the dining area like you would one indoors, but in a more relaxed fashion. Choose the mood and dress the table accordingly. Select stylish linens, fresh-cut flowers, glittering candles, and relaxed dinnerware. Use sparkling stemware to beautifully finish the setting. When creating pockets for conversation, position chairs and benches closely and provide cozy cushions and pillows for comfort. Keep accent tables within reach for guests to place their food and drink.

Outdoor living has lured cooking into the garden. In some homes, this equates to a secondary outdoor kitchen that is fully equipped with features like a refrigerator, stove, oven, and even a dishwasher. These well-appointed culinary areas should be protected from the elements and located near an entry of the home, providing easy access from the indoors. Simpler barbecue stations, designed to serve diners indoors or out, are best located near the primary kitchen inside. Large or small, the outdoor kitchen should have adequate storage space and level surfaces for preparing and serving food. The kitchen is best positioned near the outdoor dining table and surrounded with interesting surface treatments, accents, and lighting that complement the space and delights its guests.

PAGE 115
When setting the stage for outdoor dining, this casual garden calls upon "props" that make the meal special. Keeping it simple is the key here—white dishes, sparkling glassware, and comfortable furniture. Nearby jasmine fills the air with its sweet perfume and potted geraniums add color and relaxed style.

RIGHT
Imagination and an adventurous spirit are important to unlocking a dynamic outdoor dining area. This enclosed garden space is surrounded by strong architectural detail including a dramatic fireplace, stacked-stone water feature, mixed-material floor treatment, and multilevel walls that elevate the garden's contemporary style. A built-in barbecue finishes the space perfectly.

Part of the fun of outdoor garden entertaining is the opportunity to use imaginative treatments and unique touches to infuse the outdoor space with your individual style. Because most events are special and short-lived, be bold. Make the setting memorable. Combine decorative elements from indoors with lively accents from the garden. Fine linens scattered with flower petals, hurricane lamps glowing beside sparkling crystal, and luxuriously fringed pillows cushioning cast-iron chairs are just a few examples of the endless ways to make outdoors entertaining simply that—entertaining.

UPPER RIGHT
Crisp and refreshing, dress whites and crystal set the stage for an evening of fine dining outdoors. Soft layered tablecloths relax the tabletop.

LOWER RIGHT
Perfect for entertaining, separate seating areas delineate the living and dining zones of this spacious patio. The matching modern furniture and continuous flooring treatment unite the two spaces beautifully.

OPPOSITE
Position your outdoor furniture to take advantage of garden views. This bar faces the dining table, allowing those seated at the counter to enjoy the golf course vista.

It simply never fails—guests always gather in the kitchen during a dinner party. The same holds true outdoors. Today, the seated bar has become the rage indoors and outdoors as a way to welcome the guests into the cooking area, while providing a comfortable barrier between the cook and a busy food preparation area.

RIGHT
This indoor kitchen opens to an outdoor bar where guests can pony up for drinks and keep the cook company. When inclement weather threatens, locking shutters enclose the kitchen, protecting it from the elements.

OPPOSITE
This shaded outdoor kitchen incorporates a barbecue, sink, and serving bar—the perfect ingredients for successful outdoor entertaining. Comfortable barstools and a fully stocked serving cart complete the setting perfectly.

A hammock under the outstretched canopy of a shade tree, a reclining chaise along the edge of a sparkling pool, and a cozy chair propped in front of a blazing fire. The outdoors provides some of a home's most relaxing settings. What relaxes you? For some, it may be a secluded

RELAX

corner in the far reaches of the garden while others need only a cushioned chair warmed by the afternoon sun. Relaxation is highly individual. There are some elements, however, that are universally useful in elevating the pleasure of being outdoors. Foremost there is comfort. For this reason, any place you sit or recline, whether it is on a chair, chaise, daybed, or bench, the furniture should be easy and welcoming. Ample cushions and pillows up the "comfort quotient" of furnishings while boosting the style of the space with their colors, patterns, and textures. For light shelter, awnings and umbrellas can help create shade and decrease the glare of a bright day. Screens can be used to as windbreakers, adding to the serenity of the setting. Because the garden is home to many wonderful fragrances such as roses, jasmine, and rosemary for example, it seems natural to place some of these aromatic plants near a favorite resting spot. At the same time, a garden's chirping birds, tinkling wind chimes, and moving water from fountains  and pools play their music outdoors and can be used to disguise the sounds of traffic and city noise. These are just a few of the ways to create peace in the garden. Simply locate your favorite resting spot outdoors and fill it with design and detail that transform it into a restorative sanctuary.

For most people, casual equates to comfort. This certainly holds true with outdoor living. If you desire a lighthearted outdoor space, choose simple styling and natural materials. Keep the design loose and unpretentious. Formality is out of place in a relaxed garden, so display of accessories—potted plants, ceramics, pillows—should appear effortless and spontaneous. Include accents and furnishings that make you happy and colors that fit the setting's theme. Muted pastels and washed floral prints soften a Victorian's front porch wonderfully, while boldly colored stripes and solids are perfect for the deck of a beachfront cottage.

UPPER LEFT
The picnic table is the most relaxed of dining tables. Here, one of a table's benches has been replaced with canvas-backed director's chairs to heighten the overall style. A matching umbrella completes the look wonderfully.

LOWER LEFT
Whether it's a day spent sunning at the beach or puttering in the flower beds, the outdoor shower offers a relaxed and wonderful way to clean up before entering the home.

OPPOSITE
The simple use of fabric makes an outdoor room more comforting and casual. Colorful striped canvas dresses this setting with fresh summer style. Similarly shaded accessories—glassware, pillows, umbrellas, linens—add to the fun and fashion of the space.

124

> A hundred objective measurements didn't sum the worth of a garden;
> only the delight of its users did that. Only the use made it mean something.
>
> Lois McMaster Bujold

ABOVE
Away from the hustle and bustle of the house, a poolside chaise and flickering candles transform a day's end into an evening of pure bliss.

OPPOSITE
Low walls, earthy colors, and an eye-catching fireplace frame this wonderful patio with a relaxed and casual style. Every detail of the space is created to complement rather than compete with the open desert view.

If you are relaxed by a design element inside of the home, most likely it will have the same affect on you in the garden. Observe what calms and quiets you indoors, and bring it outside. If you enjoy music, install speakers on your patio, porch, or deck. If soft lighting soothes you, put a dimmer on an outdoor fixture, light candles, or add a shaded lamp to your garden's accessories. The idea is to think beyond classifying items as either "indoor" or "outdoor" and to view your garden spaces simply as an extension of your home's overall living area. As long as an outdoor area is suitably protected from the elements, or its furnishings are weather-proofed, there is no reason any treatment, object, or detail shouldn't be welcome in your personalized outdoor living room.

LEFT AND OPPOSITE
The best outdoor living rooms are designed not just for appearance, but also for practical use. This sumptuous patio relies on even the smallest details—burning candles, overstuffed cushions, chenille throw—to make it as comfortable and inviting as any space indoors.

An outdoor room most often sits between the inside of a home and the landscape that surrounds it. When designed well, an outdoor living space—whether a porch or terrace, a veranda or deck—can create a pleasing transition from within a home's interior into the garden by featuring elements from both. It harmoniously ties the two entities together and unites the design theme of the entire property. Sometimes, a common flooring material—stone, tile, scored concrete—flows indoors to out. The same is true of various wall and ceiling treatments. Color can also be used to unify the areas and can be duplicated

TRANSITIONS

through upholstery fabrics, wood finishes, surfaces, and accessories. Of course, potted plants, bordering flower beds, and water features, can be used to tie the outdoor living area to the gardens. Like a middleman, the outdoor living space takes beautiful qualities from both the home and landscape uniting the two entities gracefully.

Perhaps the most striking quality of a beautiful home is its "fit." The landscape fits the geographical setting, the home fits the landscape and the outdoor living spaces tie them all together. In a well-designed home, the details that exist indoors influence and interact with those of the landscape and exterior living areas. This symbiotic relationship between of the home and its surroundings provides a basis for harmonious design.

PAGE 131
Sliding floor-to-ceiling windows are all that separate the "in" and "out" of this stunning home. The outdoor living and pool areas feature the same stone flooring, bold architecture, and stylishly fashioned, large scale furnishings as the interior. This unified approach expands the overall living area of the property and is in keeping with its strong clean-lined design.

OPPOSITE AND RIGHT
This western home's comfortably furnished porch and entry are so at one with both its natural setting and the home's interior that it is hard to tell where the living space ends and nature begins. The porch's plank decking, heavy beam work, and lantern sconces perfectly complement the warm wood tones and rustic finishes found inside the home.

LEFT AND ABOVE
A floor-level fire feature, rock-walled grotto, and private patio lure the eye from inside a hallway and neighboring bedroom into this man-made desert oasis. The same stone features fabricated outdoors are repeated above an interior stone fireplace and in a bedroom corner to blur the boundaries of the indoor and outdoor living areas.

OPPOSITE
Large pivoting glass doors open this home's decidedly modern interior into an equally stylish outdoor living space. Bold colors, sleek furnishings, and common concrete flooring visually unite the two areas, enlarging the home's overall living space.

Gardens and outdoor spaces become part of an interior decor when viewed from inside the home. Their details impact the room from which they are viewed. Keep this in mind when designing an outdoor space. Favor complementary surfaces, finishes, and furnishings. Also consider the view when placing objects in the outdoor area. Don't block the vista with large plants, furnishings, or screens unless, of course, you are attempting to hide or disguise an unattractive outdoor element. Think of the exterior spaces as extensions of those indoors and the detail that personalizes the inside of your home will just naturally flow to these spaces outside.

Outdoor living spaces can be just as beautiful and comfortable as their indoor counterparts. They can be as relaxed as a country porch with wicker furniture and baskets of fruit, or as stately as a formal terrace with brick floors and topiary-planted stone urns. The secret to creating your own special outdoor retreat is to lavish it with distinctive detail that draws you from inside the home and lures you into the stylish spaces and the gardens beyond.

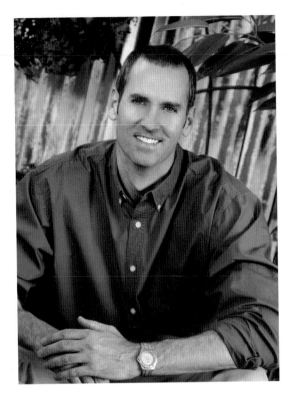

Brad Mee is a writer, author, and magazine editor who specializes in home design. *Outdoor Spaces: Design Is in the Details* is the fifth of a nationally renowned publication series he has created. It follows four other books—*Bedrooms: Design Is in the Details*, *Bathrooms: Design Is in the Details*, *Kitchens: Design Is in the Details*, and his first book *Design Is in the Details* which addresses the overall home and garden. The entire series celebrates the power of detail in creating unique and beautifully personalized spaces, indoors and out. Brad is the editor of *Utah Style & Design Magazine* and divides his time between Salt Lake City, Utah, and Phoenix, Arizona.

I would like to express my appreciation all those who made this book possible. Behind every page is the work of extremely talented people. To the creative designers, architects, builders, and manufacturers whose talents are showcased throughout the book, thank you. Your work inspires high-style outdoor living. To the extraordinary photographers who captured the beauty of these gardens and outdoor rooms, I am indebted. My gratitude also goes to the gracious home owners who welcomed us into their Eden-like outdoor oases. I am especially grateful to Don Skypeck and colleagues at Chapelle, Ltd., for their continued support and to Karmen Quinney, my skilled and dedicated editor. My appreciation goes as well to John and Margaret Mary Shuff for their enthusiastic support. I would like to recognize *Utah Style & Design Magazine* and *Phoenix Home and Garden Magazine* and for the numerous images featured that were originally seen in the publications. Finally, my sincerest thanks to photographers Dino Tonn and Scot Zimmerman for their friendships, their wonderful talents, and the contributions they made to this book.

The author would like to thank the following for contributing photography to this book:

Dino Tonn Photography
5433 East Kathleen Road
Phoenix, Arizona 85254
(602) 765-0455
An attention to detail and true artistry in lighting have made Dino Tonn one of the leading architectural photographers in the Southwest. Specializing in award-winning architectural and golf-course photography, Tonn has been photographing much of the Southwest's finest architecture for the past 13 years. He serves clients in the hospitality field as well as architects, interior designers, developers, and many other design-related businesses and publications. His work has been featured in regional and national publications. Tonn is a native of Arizona and resides in Scottsdale, Arizona, with his wife and two children.

Christiaan Blok—Photographer
(602) 667-5577
Phoenix, Arizona
www.cblok.com
A native of The Netherlands, Blok has pursued a career in Architectural and Interior photography. After graduating in 1990 from the Brooks Institute Of Photography in Santa Barbara, California he settled in Phoenix, Arizona where he is currently based. He works world wide for magazines and book projects and shoots on regular basis for *Traditional Home, Southern Accents* and *Phoenix Home & Garden*. To view current work, log on to www.cblok.com

Scot Zimmerman—Photographer
P.O. Box 289
261 North 400 West
Heber City, Utah 84032-0289
(800) 654-7897/zimfolks@sprynet.com

Scot Zimmerman is an architectural photographer. During the last 20 years, his accomplishments include: photographing and producing seven books, having his photographs featured in over 48 books, regular contributions to national and regional architectural and home & garden publications, and ongoing assignments across the country. Six museums have exhibited his work.

Paul Schatz
Interior Design Imports
San Diego, California
(619) 696-6373
Paul Schatz, principal of Interior Design Imports leads a design team recognized for consistently delivering the highest level of design expertise in an organized and professional manner. The IDI design team explores a wide range of styles with an emphasis on interior architectural detailing, bridging the gap between architect, builder, and designer.

Brown Jordan
www.brownjordan.com
(800)-743-4252
Since 1945, Brown Jordan has designed luxury outdoor furnishings and accessories that transcend time and liberate the senses. Jordan's innovative collections represent a culmination of aesthetic and reductive design methods merged with superior construction—powerful combination yielding collectible furnishings that last.

Gloster
www.gloster.com
888-GLOSTER
Gloster Furniture has a reputation built on quality, experience, and credibility. These are values that they are proud of and will always remain at the core of their business. As a leader in the Casual Furniture Industry, they know that whether you are seeking furniture for garden, patio, deck, pool or beach, you'll find endless outlets for self-expression from their range. Gloster

ACKNOWLEDGMENTS

Furniture continues to build upon their position as the premier teak supplier and they have now widened their range to include exciting new teak and metal combinations, sling groups, and all wicker collections.

Janus et Cie
www.janusetcie.com
(800)-24JANUS
Janus et Cie products add a distinctive look to the world's finest private and public settings: residences, estates, parks, gardens, hotels, libraries, shopping centers, food courts, theme parks, restaurants, universities, museums, hospitals, country clubs, fine ships and yachts. JANUS et Cie provides more than furniture. Their expert staff serves both private and professional clients with creativity and efficiency, offering elegant solutions to any design situation. JANUS et Cie has evolved gradually. Entering their 25th year of commitment to bringing the best of design and quality to their valued clients worldwide. The best furniture to sun in, dine on, or simply look at—indoors or out.

Kreiss Collection
www.kreiss.com
1-800-KREISS-1
The Kreiss Collection offers a singular blend of timeless inspiration and classic styling expressed in the finest materials, finishes, textures, fabrics and accessories. A Kreiss room mixes geographies and influences, with a style for every taste, every mood, every moment. So you enjoy infinite possibilities for customizing your home beautifully—with Kreiss.

McGuire
www.mcguirefurniture.com
1-800-662-4847
To connoisseurs of fine furniture, the name McGuire is synonymous with style and elegance. For over 50 years, McGuire Furniture Company of San Francisco has built a reputation for design and quality as gracious and lasting as the furniture it makes. Since its founding, McGuire has always handcrafted its designs of the finest materials. Given the endless combination of styles, materials, finishes and upholstery, McGuire's skilled craftsmen, artisans and tailors custom make each piece for its discerning buyer. The company's mission is to lend pleasure and permanence to contemporary living creating functional art of lasting value, backed by exceptional service.

Oldcastle Architectural, Inc.
www.belgard.biz
Old Castle Architectural, Inc. is comprised of five major product groups including concrete block, pavers, patio blocks, ornamental concrete, brick, packaged cement mixes and roof tile. Located in Atlanta, Georgia, Oldcastle APG operates as one division of Oldcastle, Inc., the leading producer of aggregates and concrete products in the United States.

Restoration Hardware
www.restoration.com
At Restoration Hardware, you'll explore an exceptionally well-merchandised world of high quality textiles, furniture, lighting, bathware, hardware and amusements. These are products of lasting value, classic design and imbued with a brand that speaks to superb taste and a free spirited individual.

Tuscan Garden Works
www.tuscangardenworks.com
Making garden rooms inside and out, transporting you to far away places, that's what Tuscan Garden Works does best. The Showroom is a display of quality built structures, all powdercoat finished, and multifunctional. Custom-design iron details range from gazebos to quilt rocks, European window boxes to castle fireplace screens.

Hob Knob Inn
www.hobknob.com
(800) 696-2723
A small luxury inn with country house ambience and service located in the heart of historic Edgartown, MA

CREDITS

PHOTOGRAPHY

Christiaan Blok 2, 17, 24, 25

Dino Tonn 11, 19, 27, 30(lr), 37, 39, 44–45, 49, 50, 52, 53(ur, lr), 55(r), 59–60, 70, 72(lr), 73, 78–79, 84–85, 89, 102, 105–109,112–113, 116–117, 119, 128–129, 132–133, 135

Jessie Walker 5, 12–13, 43, 51, 63, 80

Scot Zimmerman 3, 6(l, r) 8, 18(ur), 23(l), 34(ul), 40(ur), 47–48, 53(ll), 56–58, 61(ul,lr), 64–66, 68–69, 71(ul,ur,lr), 72(ur), 74–75, 76(l), 77, 82(ll), 83, 94(l), 100, 101(ur), 110, 111(ctr, r), 118(lr), 120–121, 127, 134

Brad Mee (photostylist) 18(lr), 61(lr), 65, 74–75, 76(l), 77, 111(l), 118(lr), 127, 134

Margie Van Zee (photostylist) 49, 50(r), 89, 128-129, 135

INTERIOR DESIGN

Anne Gale, Wiseman & Gale Interiors, Scottsdale, AZ 11 ,70, 84–85

Billi Springer Interior Design, Scottsdale, AZ 27

Brad Mee, Phoenix, AZ 52

Dale Gardon Design, Scottsdale, AZ 132–133

Electoria Electric Inc., Phoenix, AZ 107

Est. Est., Scottsdale, AZ 128–129

Friedman & Shields Interiors, Scottsdale, AZ 105

Glenn Farner, GEF Development, Scottsdale, AZ 108–109

Interior Design Imports, San Diego, CA Paul Schatz 6(ctr), 46(lr), 62, 136–137

Ivana Maschi 37, 55(r)

Jamie Herzlinger Interiors, Phoenix, AZ 102

Jennifer Hoage, Christalie Interiors, Phoenix, AZ 50(r)

Jill Kellerman, Robb & Stucky, Scottsdale, AZ 112–113

Jill Jones and Sherrie Thompson, St. George, UT 18(ur), 74, 76, 134

Jim Felter, Hasbrook Interiors, Scottsdale, AZ 89

Joe Pitti and Mark Chambers, Salt Lake City, UT 34(ul)

Kim Fisher Colletti, Treken Interiors, Scottsdale, AZ 119

Nancy Fournier, Phoenix AZ 12(ll), 42(ctr)

Paula Den Boer, Scottsdale, AZ 78

Peter Magee, Scottsdale, AZ 19

Shellie Rudow, Shellie Rudow Interiors, Chandler, AZ 106

Teresa DeLellis Design Assoc., Carefree, AZ 60

ARCHITECTS

Alan Tafoya AIA, Carefree, AZ 27

Andrew Wright, Rancho Santa Fe, CA 6(ctr), 46(lr), 62, 136–137

Craig Stoffel, CCBG Architect, Phoenix, AZ 79

Dale Gardon Designs, Scottsdale, AZ 132–133

Denis Kurutz, Landscape Architect, Pasadena, CA 6(ctr), 46(lr), 62, 136-137

Eddie Jones, Jones Studio, Phoenix, AZ 47(ll), 135

Garden Craft, Phoenix, AZ 52(lr), 116-117

H&S International, Scottsdale, AZ 78

Michael Glassman, Landscape Architect, CA 8, 58

Peter M. Magee, Scottsdale, AZ 19

R. J. Bacon Co., Phoenix, AZ 60

Randall Fonce Architects, Phoenix, AZ 30(r)

Rick Daugherty, Scottsdale, AZ 49

Shelby Wilson Architect, Carefree, AZ 37, 55(r)

Wes Balmer, Phoenix, AZ 11, 70, 84-85

KEY
(l) = left
(r) = right
(u) = upper
(l) = lower
(ctr) = center

BUILDERS

Arnette-Romero Builders, Scottsdale, AZ 27

Cal Christiansen Custom Homes, Scottsdale, AZ
11, 59, 70, 84–85

DeLellis Development Group, Carefree, AZ 60

GEF Development, Scottsdale, AZ 108–109

Geoff Edmunds Custom Homes, Scottsdale, AZ
52(lr), 116–117

Homebuilder's Group, Phoenix, AZ 39

Kitchell Custom Homes, Phoenix, AZ 128–129

Magee Custom Homes, Scottsdale, AZ 19

Moenkopi Construction, St. George, UT 18(lr),
74, 76, 134

Paragon Custom Homes, Scottsdale, AZ 44–45

MPK Holdings, LLC, St. George, AZ 75, 127

Phoenix Smith Builders, Scottsdale, AZ 105

Ray Jung, contractor, Del Mar, CA 6(ctr), 46(lr), 62,
136–137

Shiloh Custom Homes, Scottsdale, AZ 78

Stone Cliff Development, St. George, UT 61(lr)

PRODUCT

Brown Jordan 22(ur), 55(l), 142

Gloster 30(ur), 31, 41, 42(r), 90–91, 114–115, 126

JANUS et Cie 15(ur), 18(ul), 40(lr), 54(l), 61(ll),
86–87, 92–93, 104, 118(ur), 124–125, 144

Kreiss Collection 28–29, 67, 122, 130–131

McGuire 7(r), 14–15, 95, 139

Oldcastle Architectural, Inc. 42(l)

Restoration Hardware 1, 76(r), 82(lr)

Tuscan Garden Works, Salt Lake City, UT 81, 82(ul)

Ward & Child—The Garden Store, Salt Lake City,
UT, Jerry Stanger and Rob McFarland 68

RESORTS/HOTELS

Hob Knob Inn, Edgartown, MA 35

Royal Palms, Scottsdale AZ 16

Torre di Bellosguardo, Florence, Italy 26

PHOTODISKS

Photodisc, Inc. Images (© 1999) 7(ctr), 18(ur), 21,
23(ur), 32, 34(ll), 38, 46(ul, ll), 72(lr), 88, 94 (l,r),
97,98–99, 101(ul,ll,lr), 103, 123, 143

Getty Images 20, 22(lr), 23(lr), 33, 71(ll), 96

Every effort has been made to credit all contributors. We apologize in advance for any unintentional omission and would be pleased to insert the appropriate acknowledgment in any subsequent edition.

Almost any garden, if you see it at just the right moment,
can be confused with paradise.

Henry Mitchell